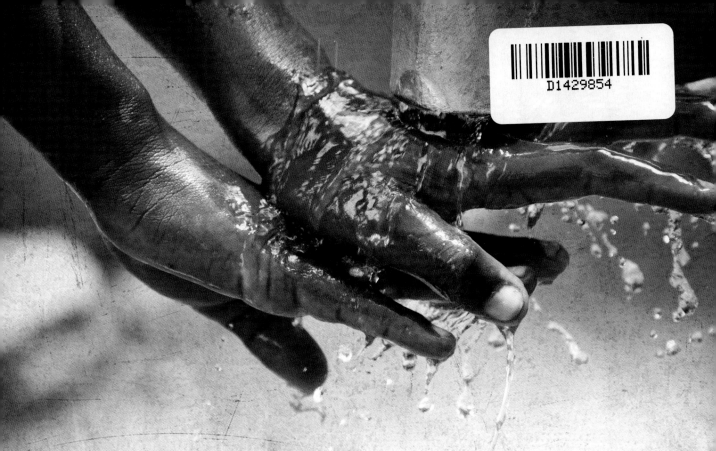

# Like Breath and Water

## PRAYING WITH AFRICA

CIONA D. ROUSE

UPPER
ROOM BOOKS®
NASHVILLE

Cover and interior design: David Uttley  /  www.luminescentimages.com
Cover image: David Uttley
First printing: 2009
Ciona D. Rouse took all photos in this volume, with the following exceptions:
David Uttley: cover, 87, 93
Cary Graham: 44
Austin Flack: 4, 10, 24, 26, 30, 33, 34, 40, 41, 45, 50, 55, 56, 83

For more information about Pray With Africa: www.praywithafrica.org

LIBRARY OF CONGRESS CATALOGING-IN-PUBLICATION DATA

Rouse, Ciona D.
   Like breath and water : praying with Africa / Ciona D. Rouse.
       p. cm.
ISBN 978-0-8358-1012-8
1. Prayer—Africa. 2. Prayer—United States. 3. Prayer—Christianity. 4. Prayers. I. Title.
   BV210.3.R68 2009
242.0967—dc22                                                                                    2009027424

Printed in the United States of America

# CONTENTS

*"If you want to learn to pray, go to Africa."*

oel's words shaped the journey for me. The expatriated Malawian said that if we were interested in learning about oil, then maybe we should visit the Middle East. Oil runs deep in their ground. But learning to pray requires a trip to a place where prayer runs beneath it all.

So we went to Africa. Austin Flack, Cary Graham, and I embarked on a short journey together for PRAY WITH AFRICA, prepared to learn about prayer, hear the prayers of the people, and record their stories. And just as the oil that fuels our cars runs deep beneath the ground in the Middle East, we learned that the prayers that fuel our hearts—our very survival—run deep in the soul of Africa. Prayer, for the people I met, does not simply petition God for the latest iGadget or beg for a quick fix to a real problem. For all of us prayer is a life force, like breath and water. Our ability to communicate with God is one way to know that we are alive.

With every prayer and prayer request we heard in Africa, we uncovered a story. These prayers revealed the hearts of the people and their lives. I was no longer a stranger who shook their hands and walked away; I was invited into a vulnerable part of their story.

As a result, I tapped into vulnerable places in my life, as well. I reached into my story and wrestled with how God calls me to live. I fell more faithfully in love with prayer.

I noticed a quotation by Oswald Chambers written on the wall of a nonprofit office in Gulu, Uganda: "Prayer does not equip us for greater works—prayer *is* the greater work."[1] Could it be that the greatest calling God has given to us is the call to be in conversation with our Creator? Could it be that we need prayer just like we need breath and water?

In these pages, I invite you to join our African pilgrimage. Through a series of vignettes, you will hear my thoughts and my wrestling and also meet some of the people who taught me how to pray with Africa.

Peace,

Ciona

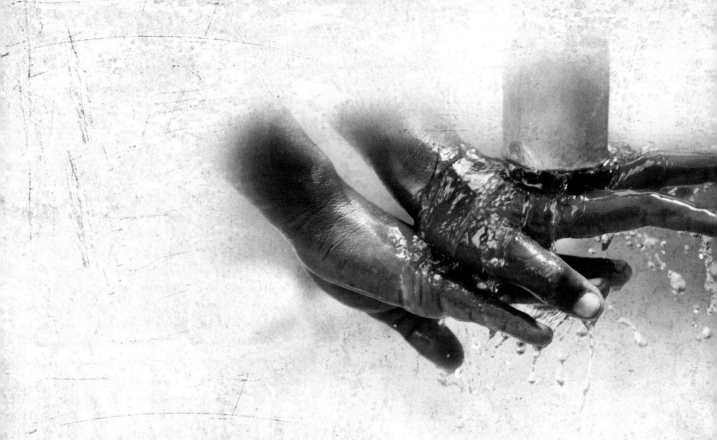

# Like Breath and Water

*I'm falling more deeply in love with prayer.*

—20 November 2008, Journal Entry

# Community

*Do I dare believe in a God*
*who might transform a place*
*simply because people around the world*
*join them in prayer?*

—8 November 2008, Journal Entry

*The only way we can ever be human is together. The only way we can be free is together.*

—ARCHBISHOP DESMOND TUTU

he air in Mali picked up orange dust from the ground and held it, producing an orange haze even at night. It greeted us when we stepped off the plane in Bamako, Mali's capital city. I took a deep breath and surveyed the land, the muted lights against the ebony sky, and the group of Malians waiting for visitors to deplane. I was in Africa.

Peter, a pastor in Mali, met Austin, Cary, and me at the airport, ready to help us learn Mali's story. Although originally from Ghana, Peter chose to live in Mali so that he could serve the people there. His church members worship God by putting feet to every song they sing, every scripture they read, and every prayer they pray. And their feet carry them into the community to love their neighbors.

Ninety percent of all Malians practice Islam, so Peter and his congregation are among the religious minority. They seem unfazed by this faith difference, even though many people in the world fear other religions. Religious persecution is no stranger in parts of Africa and other continents of the world. But against the backdrop of minarets and daily calls to prayer, Peter and his members eat with, laugh with, and serve their Muslim brothers and sisters.

*I had seen* starving children only on TV: emaciated children with swollen bellies that filled the screen while '80s rock stars sang, motivating viewers to care for the world. I've seen them more recently in videos and commercials from various relief organizations.

So as I held Kofiné in my arms in the courtyard bounded on one side by the decrepit building where her family squats (occupies property one does not own), I went into sensory overload. Four-month-old Kofiné rested peacefully in my arms, perhaps not having the strength to cry. I wrapped my pinkie around her arm and touched the palm of my own hand. Her eyes sank into her forehead. How could blood, or even breath, manage to squeeze through such a tiny frame?

We had planned to meet Kofiné and her twin sister, but her twin died four days before we arrived. The parents had no money to feed either twin. The mother, malnourished and ill, had no more breast milk.

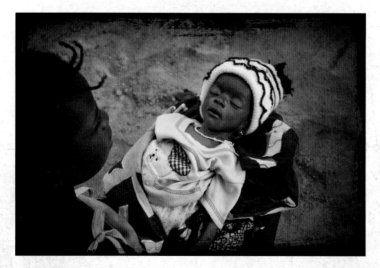

Only four days after saying good-bye to their daughter, the family exhibited an eerie calm that whispered death's familiarity. In a country where the infant mortality rate ranks among the ten highest in the world, I imagine survival becomes more surprising than death.

Other Mali mothers handed their fragile babies to me to hold, to feel the weight of their starvation. The smallness sits heavy upon my heart. One mother nudged her children toward me, using a bit of English, "You take home."

PRAY WITH MARIAM

I am from Mali in West Africa. Of course, we have a lot of prayer requests for Africa because Africa is facing a turning point, and this is a time where we talk about global things, global issues. My main concern for Africa is to pray for peace and to pray for unity.

—MARIAM

Many Malian mothers prayed that they might be able to feed their children and send them to school. They asked us not to forget them.

Archbishop Desmond Tutu of South Africa writes a lot about the African philosophy of *ubuntu*, meaning "I am who I am because of who you are." He calls it "me, we." This way of living suggests that our well-being depends on the well-being of others. We are all intertwined in one another's story. We are all a part of each other's communities despite our seeming differences. Now that I have held these mothers' children, know these women are my neighbors, and am aware that my ability to thrive depends on their ability to survive, how can I forget them?

*A five-year-old boy* walks around like a zombie. He doesn't smile. He doesn't play. When he's not being bathed or sleeping on his father's lap, he barely moves, mustering what little energy his malaria-stricken body possesses. Malaria is easily treated if you can afford medical care and healthy food. Sidibé, the boy's father, cannot afford either.

Sidibé appears stoic. His lean face never reveals his secrets. He works tirelessly every day collecting items to sell and running an informal shop next to the house where his family squats. He cannot afford his son's health care, nor can he afford to feed his family. His baby daughter, Kofiné, potentially faces the same fate as her twin sister if he cannot provide for the family.

One of Africa's financially poorest countries, 75 percent of Malians live on about a dollar a day.[2] Rising fuel costs in the last few years have affected food prices. Malians who already exist on the brink of survival silently succumb to malnutrition more and more each day.

✑

*Peter and his wife, Comfort,* serve one congregation in Bamako, and Nema is a faithful member of another congregation. Together, they have created a porridge recipe that is inexpensive, easy to make, and stores well. They travel throughout the city and the surrounding villages offering a premixed recipe and teaching people how to make it themselves.

Peter, Comfort, and Nema are not wealthy but faithful. Their faith calls them to serve their neighbors. Peter needs to send his children to school; his church needs a building in which to worship; and he has a long list of very real needs. Still he does not ignore his neighbors in order to fulfill his own needs. It's not a risk he's willing to take. So with what they have to offer and the blessings God has given them, they serve their neighbors.

*I walked through* the gates of the orphanage, past a colorful playground into a small courtyard where tiny feet shuffled toward me. Tiny hands extended up to reach mine.

Tiny voices asked me how my day was, "Ça va, mademoiselle?"

About fifteen small children shook my hand and welcomed me into their home. They all sleep, eat, and learn in this one building under the care and guidance of Gladys. I went to the orphanage alone, with no translator. Gladys spoke very little English, and I knew only a few words of French. I was going to need a Pentecost moment to get through the day.

I tried to explain, using my broken French, why I had come to Bamako. The older children looked at one another and traded stifled giggles at my expense. My simple request for their prayers seemed a confusing babble about nothing at all. I was so nervous that I might spend the entire day with these amazing children but not be able to hear a single prayer request to bring back home. Just as I began to feel defeated using French words, gestures, and pointing, the children closed their eyes and bowed their heads. Each prayed aloud for Africa and for children in the United States. Somehow they understood me! Just like that, my Pentecost moment arrived.

One by one the children stood in front of the class and shared their prayer requests with me. Aissa, an eleven-year-old with long legs and a sunshine smile, wants to be a doctor when she's older. She works hard and does well in school. Tchecna, the ten-year-old whose bright eyes and shy maturity immediately stole my heart, wants to be a preacher one day. Without knowing each other's languages, we ate together, played together, and prayed together.

In the biblical account of the tower of Babel and the tale of how languages spread throughout the world, it says that God "confused the language of all the earth." Although I rejoice in the good day I had in the orphanage, I know that building real community requires knowing each other's languages. No wonder so much conflict exists in the world. It's difficult enough to seek understanding when communicating within the same language. We're an entire world of people confused by one another until we find a real way of learning each other's languages and ways of life.

*Our last evening* in Mali, a woman named Mariam came to share a meal with Jean-Baptiste and Marie-Therese, the owners of the guesthouse where we stayed. Mariam had studied in Kenya and spoke English very well. We were relieved! We didn't have to rely on my rusty French or on Peter's translation abilities. We could speak to one another and begin to learn more about each other.

Before our evening ended, Mariam said that she wanted to pray with us—for our journey on the continent and for then President-elect Obama. We had arrived in Mali on election day in the United States, so news of our election was fresh on everyone's mind. One man told me that he stayed up all night watching the election returns and still went to work the next morning. This particular election was, indeed, historic and significant, especially for Africans. It became clear, however, throughout the journey that people regularly followed United States events, even before this historic election.

I was humbled by Mariam's graciousness to us and to the United States. I didn't know the date of the next Malian election. I didn't even know the current president's name. I certainly wasn't praying for his leadership. And it wasn't the United States alone; throughout the continent I learned how much the people I met paid attention to the politics and events in the rest of the world.

Our existence in the United States impacts their existence. We survive and thrive because of other parts of the world as well, even though we tend to think of our country as an isolated place. We are a part of each other's global community; and community, to the people we met in Africa, carries real meaning and responsibility.

*Creator of all, Author of all living things,*
*thank you for writing us into each other's story.*
*Thank you for giving us hands and feet*
*to serve alongside and walk with our neighbors.*
*Thank you for challenging us to love you by loving your people.*

*Lord, your children hunger for you.*
*We hunger for your mercy and compassion.*
*We thirst for your hope and salvation.*
*Nurture emaciated spirits.*

We need the Bread of Life to fuel our souls.

Your people hunger, Lord.

Hear the prayer of the mother whose breasts have run dry,

who holds a sickly child,

praying for the miracle that will keep her breathing.

Hear the prayer of the father whose back is bent

from working long hours for small coins

so that he might feed at least one open mouth.

Give her strength. Give him hope.

Hear the prayer of the young child

whose parents were stolen by death,

who hungers for education and dreams of a future

in a place where the ring of death's bell is far too familiar.

Hear the prayer of the faithful who love you, God,

and who love your people.

Keep them dreaming. Keep them near.


In Christ. Amen.

Hear the prayer of the young child
        whose parents were stolen by death,
who hungers for education and dreams of a future
        in a place where the ring of
death's bell is far too familiar.

# Patience

When my prayers remain unanswered,
do I commit to continual prayer
about the same thing?
Do I persevere because I believe
so deeply in God's ability to hear prayer?

—11 November 2008, Journal Entry

*The seeker-of-all things-from-God does not yield to impatience.*

YORUBA OF NIGERIA PROVERB

Our first night in the village of Awasi in the Nyanza Province of Kenya, Cary, Austin, and I went to sleep rather early. It was difficult to get much rest on the long and bumpy ride from Nairobi. I didn't mind the ride; I liked watching zebras nibbling grass on the roadside, the yellow bushes and purple trees in the distance, the miles of tea plantations, and some of the brightest green foliage I had ever seen. So we decided to crash after eating a meal with our host, Bishop Ogam, and his family.

I awoke later that night to the deep consistency of a bass voice singing a song in the Luo language. A chorus of voices echoed. It sounded as if the bishop was leading a full worship service in the next room, but the only congregants were his wife, Lucy, and their children.

I could not understand the lyrics to their songs or the words they prayed, but I quieted myself and listened to them pray and sing each night we spent in Kenya. I was invited to join them and felt welcomed when I did, but I mostly favored lying still with my eyes closed and listening to the cadence of their praise and prayer as I drifted to sleep.

They were faithful in their evening offering. Without fail, they gathered each night to thank God, praise God, and petition God.

My favorite scripture is found in Romans: "Rejoice in hope, be patient in suffering, and persevere in prayer" (12:12). Bishop Ogam and his family put flesh on this text for me.

## PRAY WITH "LUCY"

I thank you, Lord. I call upon you. I call upon your guidance.

I put all my household and my home into your hands.

O Lord, I put into your hands my husband and all the community around. Open ways and means for my husband on how he can feed my family and the community at large.

I put our Awasi Central—my church—into your hands.

Lord, you blessed everyone in it. I glorify your name, Lord.

I ask you to bring us water into Awasi, O Lord.

O God, I ask all in the name of Jesus, your son. Amen.

—"LUCY"

*Mary stood with her* toes just inches away from the murky pond water. We followed her to this spot where she and her children gather water in school-bus-yellow jugs. They carry the water a half mile back home for bathing, cleaning food, and drinking. The water is unsafe for any of these activities.

We walked a path to the pond, following a thin stream of water running over thick brown mud. Some trash that will never make it to a can decorated the stream. With no filter and no indoor plumbing, I'm certain human waste made its way to this water as well.

This is the water that Mary and more than a billion other people in the world's most impoverished countries access each day. It's the water Mary hopes will no longer make her children ill with cholera, typhoid, malaria, or bilharzia. She prays daily that the God who was powerful enough to part the Red Sea might make their water clean.

"Mary, the water has been this way for as long as you can remember, right?" I asked her.

"Yes."

"And you've been asking God for clean water for many years, right?"

"Yes."

"How, then, do you continue to pray for this when it seems that your situation stays the same?" I could not help but ask.

With a smile that matched the brilliance of her soul, Mary began to teach me how to pray. She said that she has witnessed God's miracles in her life before. She trusts God's faithfulness and persists in prayer. Even though the water has remained murky and her children and grandchildren have often gotten sick, Mary believes God hears her prayer.

How do I teach my heart this kind of prayer that keeps records of miracles instead of marking each pain caused by abandoned prayers and unfulfilled desires? How do I pray with the patience of Elijah on a mountaintop withstanding strong winds, earthquakes, and fires until the gentle whisper of God is finally heard (1 Kings 19:11-12)?

Mary thirsts for clean water. I thirst for Mary's patience.

*I received tons* of advice before traveling to Africa. One of the most common pieces of advice: throw time to the wind while in Africa. The African people, I was warned, don't operate by the watch or the calendar in the same way we do in the United States.

I'm not a fan of gross generalizations, especially when referencing an entire continent of millions of very different people. Sure, we had our share of six-hour bus rides that were supposed to have been four hours, noon beginnings to events planned at 8:00 a.m., and thirty-minute waits after being assured something would take "only a minute" to complete. We also stepped off planes exactly on time, greeted by people who had been early in anticipation of our arrival. Some mornings our hosts waited patiently for us to gather our things because they were ready early. We even received a printed itinerary for the week from our host in Malawi. I struggle to call tardiness "the African way."

I did learn a new concept of timing while traveling the continent. The "don't hurry; be happy" mentality challenged my faith. The people I encountered had an enormous amount of patience with God; when it came to trusting God's promises, my new friends waited faithfully for God to deliver. Without hurry or worry, they simply prayed and followed God's timing day by day.

*Tears fell softly from* cheek after cheek after cheek.

As the sky began saying good-bye to the sun, the women came to me, one by one, to share their prayers in front of Mary's house.

Typically, I used my tiny handheld recorder to collect lists of people's prayer requests. My invitation to hear people list their prayer requests, however, somehow got lost between English and Luo, so these women were approaching me to actually pray. One at a time, they walked toward me and, with eyes closed, invited me to record their intimate conversations with God.

Every woman—even the young girls—humbly began their prayers by giving tremendous thanks and praise to God.

"I thank you, the God of gods. I thank you for bringing us here to talk to you."

"My heart blesses you this evening, my God."

"I want to thank you, O God, who brought me out of the night."

They petitioned God for miracles:

"Provide my parents with ways and means so that they can get us food."

"I do cry to you that you do a miracle to me on my sickness."

"We have a lot of starvation; we have lack of water, but you have everything."

As the women prayed, tears escaped many of their eyelids. Praying took them to a vulnerable place where they recognized God's power and were humbled by God's ability to hear them. They were genuine tears of deep gratitude and deep pleading—the kind of tears I release when something is so great or so difficult that I'm too whelmed to hold my tears hostage.

Their tears flowed like cleansing rain.

*Something was wrong.* I shivered outdoors under Kenya's blazing sun. I could not keep food on my stomach for long. I could never get comfortable at night, and I cleared the path to the outhouse more times than I would have liked. So as I lay there wide-eyed and frustrated one night, I sought solace in the few tunes I had on my iPod. Listening to Mary's prayer about water reminded me of the song "Gratitude" by Nichole Nordeman that I hadn't heard in a long time. In this song, Nordeman begs God to send rain to a very dry and thirsty earth. Then she thanks God for the warmth of the sun and the lessons learned about thirsting for God even if the rain does not come.

Could this also be the secret to Mary's patience? Does she pray, pleading to God, while also expressing tremendous gratitude for what God provides for her already? When we gratefully thank God for the lessons learned through the seemingly ignored prayers, does this allow us to wait more patiently before God?

When I visited South Africa in 2005 and got sick, I became increasingly frustrated with my body's slow recovery and decided to return to the States earlier than planned. But this time I spent more than two weeks of our journey with various stages of illness. I'm grateful to have lessons in patience on this trip so that I could press through sleepless nights and fevers, learning a small fraction of what it means to be grateful for life even when it feels unbearable.

God of life and death,

rain and drought,

feast and famine,

I glorify your name above all names.

Thank you for breathing life into your creation.

And thank you for the intimate invitation

to be in conversation with you.

Thank you for needs supplied

and lessons learned from needs denied.

Thank you for being able to handle our
cries of why, how long, and when?
When so much of your world suffers,
how do you not use your power to make
all things new?
How long will your people have to beg
for clean water?
How long must your people long for relief?
When will you answer the cry of the needy?

Thank you for the gentle whispers
that remind us that you have never forsaken
your people.
Send more still waters than violent winds,
more candlelight than fires,
more hope than despair.
But remain close to us through it all,
so that we see you and glorify your name
all of the days we live on this earth.

Amen.

# Forgiveness

*I wanted to hold Pamela*
*and erase her painful memories.*
*I wanted to get back for her*
*what he had stolen.*
*What monstrous behavior!*
*And yet, Christ has forgiven him already.*

—20 November 2008, Journal Entry

*God does not share our hatred, no matter what the offense we have endured.*

—ARCHBISHOP DESMOND TUTU

Pamela is sixteen years old. She lives in Gulu, Uganda, at the Zion Project's Zion House.[3] She breast-feeds a sweet little girl, no more than two years old, named Maria. She does not know Maria's dad. Three young men followed Pamela and a friend on their way home from a program and raped them. Maria was born nine months later. Lord, have mercy. Christ, have mercy.

I asked Pamela for her prayer request, the things she wanted people around the world to pray with her. Pamela asked that we pray with her to learn to forgive her rapist. Lord, have mercy. Christ, have mercy.

The evening after Pamela shared her prayer request with me, I wrote in my journal about the rapist, calling his actions monstrous. He is not a monster, though. I wish I could make sense of his actions by chalking it up to a deed of nightmares and fairy tales. I wish I could dismiss him as someone created by make-believe and evil. But he was created by God and is not a monster. Pamela, whose mother is HIV-positive, cares for her entire family and is unable to return to school. She could pray for anything in the world, and her first prayer is to release the bitter root she has against her rapist.

Just as Christ has stretched wide his arms as an act of forgiving me for my sins, God has already forgiven the rapist as well. Pamela desired to be more like Christ, to remove this dreadful sin from her burden. Lord, have mercy. Christ, have mercy.

PRAY WITH PAMELA

My name is Pamela. When I was fourteen years old, I was raped.
I conceived and got this child I'm holding right now.
I still feel a bit of pain because of the rape, so I ask that you continue praying for me
that I may have a total release of the person who raped me.
I pray for my mom who is now living positively with HIV/AIDS. My daughter and I
are the only two in the family who are not HIV-positive, and this is a really big issue.
You need to pray for our family.

—PAMELA

*Mama Shekinah is like* a pied piper. As soon as you enter her presence, you want to draw nearer to her. When I met her, she stood tall and lean with slightly storied skin. Her smile challenged the Ugandan sun. Her long blond locks were pulled away from her face into a ponytail. Her daughter, Shekinah, peered around Mama's leg, one thumb in her mouth and the other hand securely fastened to Mama's hand.

Mama Shekinah was born in Paraguay and named Hedwig, and commonly called Hedi. After serving in missions for ten years, Hedi married Colin, a man from Bermuda who wanted to become a pastor. Together they discerned a calling to teach reconciliation and serve in ministry and mission in the war-torn east African countries.

On one of their journeys, the pair had just passed from Uganda into Sudan, when the Lord's Resistance Army (LRA) ambushed them. This rebel militia has wreaked havoc on northern Uganda for more than twenty years, attacking the villages of the Acholi people and mercilessly beating, abducting, or  murdering others who got in the way, even in southern Sudan. They are infamous for abducting children and forcing them to be soldiers.

The soldiers attacked Colin and Hedwig, who was three months pregnant. Though they spared her life, the young soldiers brutally murdered Colin. She remembers holding her husband, who was bruised, bloody, and barely breathing, and looking into the eyes of the soldiers. They were children, one a female. In that moment, when life as she knew it was stripped from her, Hedwig firmly decided that she must forgive these young soldiers for murdering her husband.

For almost two years, Hedwig nursed her wounds and regained her health. Six months after Colin's death, she gave birth to Shekinah, the daughter she and Colin named before his death. It means "the dwelling presence of God" in Hebrew. Then she and Shekinah returned to Africa, this time to dwell in northern Uganda in a home with young girls—former child soldiers of the LRA.

These girls, who had been pulled from their homes and trained to murder, affectionately call Hedwig "Mama Shekinah." Her home became their home.

*I saw two little boys* rolling on the ground. I tiptoed toward them, camera in hand, to capture their giggles without them posing for me. I can still hear their giggles—so sweet and innocent.

Behind me, a woman stood next to Benson, a trauma therapist who visits many camps for Internally Displaced Persons (IDP). She told her story aloud to a group of people who had gathered in the Awer IDP camp. The LRA had invaded her home, murdered her husband in front of her, and taken the children. Her pain was tremendous. How does she find healing from this kind of memory?

Before me, however, two precious boys shared quite a contagious giggle while rolling on the ground.

These children were in this camp because their families were forced out of their homes by the LRA. The burden of their families' memories could weigh them down for life. These boys may have witnessed horrific sights themselves. They could embrace a permanent despair, but their laughter sang of hope. As they tumbled on the ground, the woman beside Benson finished her story. She did not end her story in anger and revenge; she ended it with forgiveness. For her, there was no other way to find peace except in forgiveness.

Desmond Tutu says there is "no future without forgiveness." I look at these boys, and I know it's true.

*We walked many long* and dusty roads in Gulu, lined with mostly eaten corn husk remains, trampled plastic bottles, and deserted shoe soles. The walks were always longer than they seemed. Even boda-boda (motorbike taxi) rides took more time than I initially thought they would. The course was bumpy and sometimes a little frightening.

I don't want to paint a pretty picture of forgiveness—especially in a war-torn place. I think even the simple declarations of forgiveness and prayers for forgiveness that we heard in Gulu were steps on a very long road. This road is filled with painful debris—memories that will embitter and frustrate once again. Many hardships and unexpected bumps may make the course of forgiveness frightening at times. This process may take longer than any of the forgivers imagined when they first chose forgiveness.

In the end, though, it's the most beautiful road if you choose to take it. And the first sign of beauty begins in the choosing.

"Father, forgive them; for they do not know what they are doing" (Luke 23:34).

*Stella could reasonably* justify anger and revenge from any one instance on the long list of injustices she's accrued since childhood. Her father abandoned her family, so she sought solace and funding in an older man who promised to care for her. At age fourteen, she was pregnant with the first of his four children. He eventually left her as well, taking two of the children with him. Stella lost her sister to the LRA when the guerilla army killed her, leaving Stella to care for her sister's three children. Her unfortunate childhood kept her from getting an education; her only option was to brew alcohol in the IDP camp to make money to feed the children and send them to school.

On top of her own hardships, Stella lives with women who all have their share of tragic stories. They were raped or abducted. They are HIV-positive. One is not welcome at home because she was abducted by the LRA when she was twelve and forced to be one of the wives of the abominable rebel leader Joseph Kony. It's enough to forever obscure the road to forgiveness.

So I appreciate Stella's prayer:

"I want you to pray specifically for our region, which is northern Uganda, so that the conflict, which has been for quite a long time, that it may be the end of it now.

"Because of the conflict, we have lived in real poverty. I want you to pray that the people who are still having revenge and they're still in the bush with the rebellion . . . we just pray that they would come back and have a heart of staying together. . . . I'm grateful that together with your prayers, God will make a transformation and there will be a change in our lives."

Dear Lord,

Pain comes at us from every side.

We see wars and violence.

We hear of children—who are precious

in your sight—being raped

and killed,

being forced to rape and kill.

This is not the natural order of your world, Lord!

Pain comes at us from every side.
Fathers have been murdered.
Children have been forced to kill the
ones who carried them in their wombs.
Families disown their own.
This is not the natural order of your world.

Pain comes at us from every side.
It plants a seed of anger within us.
How can we heal this pain without revenge?
How will our oppressors know how much we hurt
if we do not hurt them in turn?
How can we let them smack our other cheek?
This is not the natural order of your world.

Help us choose forgiveness.
Sow in us seeds of reconciliation
where bitterness has taken root.
Teach us to choose forgiveness just as
you have chosen to forgive us.

In Christ. Amen.

Above all, clothe yourselves with love,
which binds everything together in perfect harmony.
And let the peace of Christ rule in your hearts,
to which indeed you were called in the one body.

—Colossians 3:14-15

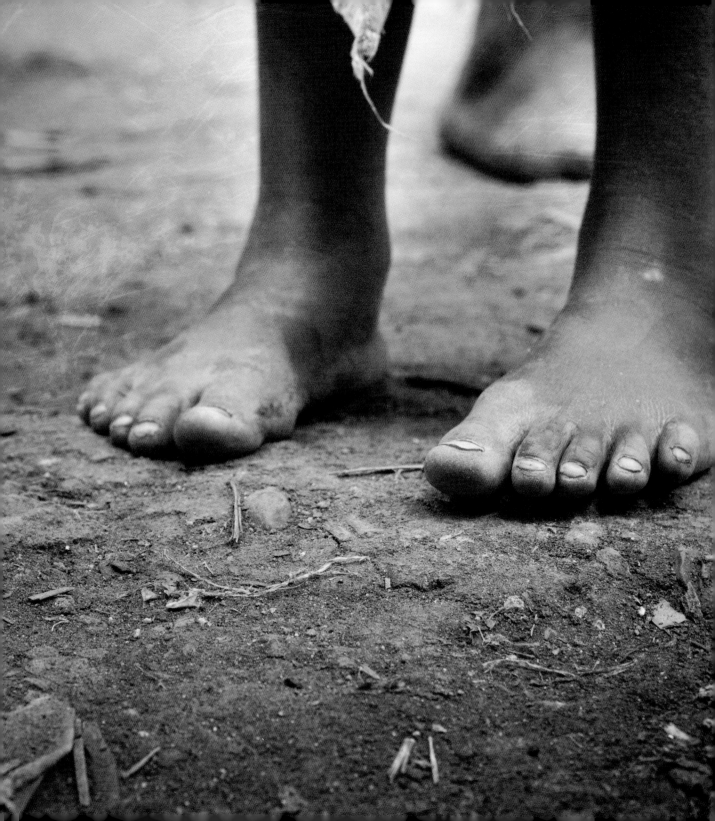

*As Malawians, we love each other.*

—Tereza of Blantyre

Some words are too powerful to use flippantly. My parents discouraged me from using the word *hate* too carelessly as a child. I wasn't allowed to hate broccoli or homework, even for a minute. "*Hate* is such a strong word," I was told. I never received reprimands when I threw around the word *love*, however. I could declare that I loved ice cream, Saturdays, and cartoons just moments after telling my parents I loved them.

*Love* is such a strong word too, and I've used it in far too many casual conversations and not enough in really hard situations with real people. I have complained far more about wrongdoings than I have turned to love the wrongdoer. I hum songs that say love is all we need, and I've watched handfuls of blissful "I dos" become regretful "I don'ts" with little warning.

We arrived in Malawi, Africa's warm heart, while violence in Congo continued to displace thousands of people. Gunmen attacked several Mumbai hotels, leaving hundreds dead or wounded. Christians and Muslims were killing one another in Nigeria. The news showed the unfortunately familiar images of war and car bombs in Iraq. I received news from home of wounded friendships and impending divorces.

The world seemed clothed in everything but love.

I breathed a deep sigh of peace and relief when I listened to the prayer requests of the people of Malawi. They prayed for love like people who believed in love's power. They did not request a flippant kind of love; they longed for a love that would end wars, stop the spread of disease, provide food for hungry mouths, and allow the church to grow.

They prayed for a love that sacrificed to make room for real Resurrection miracles.

## PRAY WITH CLAUDE

My prayer request is to pray for my financial status. I want to be blessed financially because I have an orphanage who I grant [money to] some children whose parents are dead from HIV/AIDS. I want also to pray for all the people who suffer from HIV/AIDS. I believe God can heal this disease because only God has this power for the human being.

The hospitals just care for us, but God heals.

For Africa, I want peace in Africa; and once we have peace, we can do anything, and everything will be possible. Without peace, the people who suffer HIV, we cannot reach them.

—CLAUDE

*Chisomo was a* young boy in primary school when his mother needed him most. Esther was HIV-positive, and her son did not know if she would live or die. Chisomo decided he needed to drop out of school to care for his mother day in and day out.

Now Chisomo has missed too many years of schooling to return. Having sacrificed his education, he has few options to cycle out of the poverty he and Esther face daily. Esther prays that God will help her son have a future.

*Chisomo*, in Chichewa, means "grace." Chisomo has been God's grace in the flesh for his mother.

The people of Malawi pray for love like they really believe in its power. Mothers like Esther do believe in its power because they have experienced the healing power of love. Like Mary in Kenya, they have witnessed what God can do. While some people may think their prayers for love are naïve or impractical, the Malawians base their prayers on a deep faith—a faith that trusts what God has done and believes what God will do again.

*We drove uphill* on a long dirt road, the dust from our tires settling on the conversations our passing by had sparked: Who are these *azungus* (foreigners)? What brings them here?

Claude, one of our new friends, stopped the car on the hilltop next to a brilliantly painted home where about twenty people sat in the yard. They were expecting us. We received their warm hellos through smiles, clapping, and song. "You are welcome here," they said to us.

On any given day, up to eighty people gather in this small yard in the Kampala village and sit under a short but far-reaching tree. Every day they practice welcoming. Many of the people under the tree no

longer talk to their families. Many of their spouses have died; their parents and friends have disowned them.

All under this tree have tested positive for HIV, or they love someone who is HIV-positive. They are older women and young adult men, children and babies, Christians and Muslims, northerners and southerners, widowed and married. They do not cling desperately to the pain of being ostracized by their families. They have adopted a new family, finding support, strength, and love in one another. This love does not fear the HIV diagnosis; it loves without condition.

Nearly 900,000 people in Malawi live with HIV/AIDS. Eighty of them live in this community and call themselves Tiwasunge. In Chichewa, Tiwasunge means, "Let's nurse them."

*We spent Thanksgiving Day* in Blantyre, Malawi. Not only did we not have turkey and an endless supply of optional side dishes, but we also had no desire to splurge quite as much as we typically do in the United States on this holiday. We did manage to find an Americanesque meal at Café Rouge consisting of cheeseburgers, a grilled-cheese sandwich, a milk shake, a Coke float, and two pieces of cake. We enjoyed this feast with our hosts Collings and Claude, so I explained the holiday to them.

I told them that Thanksgiving was a special holiday in the United States where most of us reflect on our thankfulness for God's blessings. I stated that we eat a lot of food on this day, and we spend time with our family. Collings seemed very happy that we had a holiday like this, and he said, "Oh! So do you visit orphans on this day, as well?"

When Collings heard about a day of gratitude and family, his concern did not focus on whether we played games or watched football. He didn't care how much food we ate or which sides were our favorites. His immediate concern was that we showed love to those who have no family.

❧

*During evening devotionals* we talked about the stories God was writing in our lives. Our new friend Sylvester told his story, which began in a village where his family worked hard for little pay on a tea plantation near the majestic Mount Mulanje. When he was older, Sylvester worked the tea grounds too and became fascinated with the earth and agriculture.

Sylvester studied agriculture in school and, from the look of his bookshelf, continues to study the earth. After managing the plantation for a while, Sylvester moved to Blantyre, many miles away from his home. Now he works for the city of Blantyre as one of the leaders who plan the city's agriculture

and greenery. The bright Flamboyant trees lining Blantyre's sidewalks—and even the sidewalks themselves—are there because of Sylvester's work. He is so grateful to be born into an aspect of agricultural life and for God to have written his story, calling him to care for creation in this way.

I was surprised by Sylvester's commitment to planning the city of Blantyre's World AIDS Day commemoration. Although the city hosted the event, HIV/AIDS, in my opinion, had little to do with Sylvester's job title.

Or maybe the two issues have stronger ties than my initial thoughts could muster. Sylvester fell in love with God's creation and felt called to care for it—*all* of creation.

I return to the Garden where our Creation narrative takes place. There we learn of God's enlivening all of creation—from soil to water to humanity. Loving the earth calls us to love people, and loving God's people begs for us to love the land we call home.

*My prayer is simple:*
*May we choose love, Lord.*
*May we choose love when faced with retaliation,*
*love when tempted by deception,*
*love when addressing poverty,*
*love when speaking to our neighbors,*
*love when lured by bad choices,*
*love when electing leaders.*
*In all the things we do, in all the words we say, and in all the places we go,*
*may we always choose love.*
*Amen.*

# Healing

Helen Johnson Hospital seemed like a place
that knew more about housing people who die than
housing people who are made well.
What is healing? Come, Lord Jesus. Amen.

—3 December 2008 Journal Entry

# COME BACK MISSION.

## ALCOHOL, DRUGS & HIV/AIDS

Tel 011·342·1662.

084·610·8072

*However long the night may last, there will be morning.*

— MOROCCAN PROVERB

n 2005, I stayed with the Pillay family in Johannesburg only weeks after their oldest daughter came back home.

Cheryl and Roy's daughter Monique lived with her drug-addicted boyfriend who needed money to feed his habit. So she stole the money from her father's growing business. Her boyfriend took the money and soon took off, leaving her with nothing.

Monique couldn't go home. How could she return to the family she had deserted and robbed? How could she dare ask them to help her? She had no other option, so she found herself bent and broken in front of the family she had deceived. They welcomed her home with open arms. It was not an easy transition; they had a number of tears and frustrations, but nevertheless they welcomed her.

The scriptures unfolded before my eyes. I imagined them saying, like the father in Luke's parable, "This daughter of ours was dead and has come back to life!" (AP)

Since then, Cheryl has created an organization with other members of the Eldorado Park community. They call it Come Back Mission. This group of people already serve their neighbors, but now they serve their neighbors *together*. They work with alcohol and drug addicts, HIV/AIDS patients, and anyone else who needs to discover healing and wholeness. Their motto: "Your setback is your comeback." Their logo is a person with arms outstretched, ready to receive.

No matter the situation or how many people have abandoned them, when people are ready to find wholeness, Cheryl and her friends rejoice like the prodigal's father saying, "Our neighbor was dead and has come back to life!" (AP)

*Joseph tasted freedom* in June 2008 for the first time in years.

He walked through the Eldorado Park community like he would on any other day. The Come Back Mission crew set up shop in a park on one of Eldorado's more prominent corners. The drug dealers were all around and on other corners. Cheryl, Bernie, Auntie Connie, and others from Come Back Mission didn't care.

This group was a direct threat to the dealers. On one corner, the dealers offered to feed the addictions of the passersby for a fee. On its corner, Come Back Mission passed out information and inspiration to help free the addicts from the hold of drugs and alcohol.

Joseph approached the women, towering over their short frames, to see what they were doing. He listened to the ladies and took their information into his thin hands and went on his way.

Joseph's long, lean legs can carry him eleven kilometers in thirty minutes. He has dreamed of running races professionally and has even run some of South Africa's local races and performed well, but the drugs were slowing him down. He craved this manufactured high more than he committed to training. Now he wanted to be free to run and chase his dreams.

So Joseph went to Come Back Mission to check out how the people could help him. There he experienced the hope of healing. Many of Come Back's leaders are trained counselors who committed to walk through the rehab process with him.

When we arrived in Johannesburg in December, Joseph had just returned from a detox center absolutely clean of drugs. He looked good, felt healthy, and was training at least twice each day. His life had been restored, but he still lived in a home with others on drugs. His community did not offer the support the people of Come Back Mission offered. His new healing meant saying good-bye not only to his habit but also to some close friends and family, and this was a real burden for Joseph.

But he had feasted on freedom, and I could see in his eyes that it whetted Joseph's appetite for more.

Pray With Africa

PRAY WITH VERONICA

I have a big problem. I was supposed to go for an operation,

but my family would not sign for it.

I want just a prayer that the pain goes away.

—VERONICA

*I remembered Laverne* from my 2005 visit in Johannesburg. Cheryl had walked a group of us through the Heavenly Valley community just outside of Soweto, passing numerous makeshift houses in this informal settlement before arriving at Laverne's place. We stood inside Laverne's small, scrap-metal home. She no longer heard from some of her friends and family members. It meant so much to her to have people from the United States inside her home so others in the community would see that it was OK to be around her. They ignored her because of her HIV-positive diagnosis.

In 2005 Laverne was small in height and weight, and she had a few mouth sores. Otherwise, you could hardly tell she was sick. She still had life and movement in her.

I saw Laverne again this visit; Cheryl took us to the hospital with Laverne's sister Charlotte to check on her. We hovered over her bed, looking down at her frail body curled beneath a caramel-colored blanket. Sores covered her lips. She used half of every muscle in her body to open her eyes for only a few seconds. She lightly whispered a few words that I could not understand because one of the three other patients in her room yelled the entire time we were there. Her CD4 (specialized cells that fight infection)

count was so low that the doctors said it was pointless to give her the antiretroviral medicines anymore. We were watching a woman dying slowly.

As we left Laverne's room, Cary looked at his watch and said, "Ciona, it's time for Bill to speak." I had sat with my friend Bill a year before in a room as the HIV test administrator told us his test had come back positive, and this memory flooded my mind. At the same moment that we said good-bye to Laverne, Bill was speaking at a chapel service the week of World AIDS Day about his experience of being HIV-positive in the United States. I was proud of his

courage to speak and heavy laden by Laverne's weakening body.

I prayed for God to heal both of them that day, but I felt defeated. What does healing look like in the face of a disease with no cure?

## What is healing?

How do we pray for it?

I know Cheryl and Roy prayed regularly for their daughter Monique to return home and be made well, and she did come home. Joseph prayed for recovery and healing, and he got it.

Charlotte has prayed for her sister's healing; but Laverne's body is weak, and AIDS is incurable.

Or could God miraculously heal her? Still, Laverne can't live forever; her death will come. So is death the *absence* of healing, or does death make *space* for healing?

The people of South Africa are healing from the painful past of apartheid. It has taken many years to reach this point; healing has come only through truth and reconciliation. It required death to an old way of life that was hated by the masses and benefited a few. This death had to happen in order for the healing process to begin.

A death to their old selves has made room for Joseph's and Monique's healing too. So when I pray for Laverne's healing, is it for a physical healing? Or will Laverne's death make room for another kind of healing to begin?

I find it hard to make sense of praying for healing. Is my prayer going to change God's mind about a situation? I don't believe that prayer is about petitioning to change God's mind; it's about a pure and honest relationship with God. It's about recognizing the imperfection of our will. When I pray for healing, I do have a desired outcome. I don't want to learn a lesson from God's yes or no; I always want a yes. I always want a physical, tangible healing. What do I do with this?

I watched Auntie Joyce knead the dough. The Come Back Mission team and their clients sang praise songs as she prepared the yeast and nurtured the lumpy dough with her hands. Then others took their turn kneading the dough and rolling it into balls to let rise.

All the while, Auntie Connie talked about the bread they were making. She said that maybe there are lumps in our lives like the ones in the dough, and we're to give them to God to knead. Maybe this process takes time; you have to sit and be patient as you wait for the bread to rise, she reminded everyone. Sometimes our prayers take a while for God to answer.

Each week Come Back Mission makes bread. The clients and leaders of the group enjoy fellowship with one another while they wait for it to rise and bake. They eat it together, and then they take some of the remaining bread to others as a reminder that all should help others even as they receive help.

The bread that day never quite came out like it should have. Something went awry in the rising process, but we placed it on the table along with a display of candles. Before eating the bread together, Cheryl invited each of us to light a candle and confess or share a prayer request. Everyone—addicts, victims, and leaders alike—shared a part of his or her story. A visitor cried as she openly acknowledged her recent HIV-positive diagnosis to people she did not know.

*Thank you, God, for having a plan far greater than anything we can imagine.*

*You bring down walls of injustice that we build.*

*You loosen chains of addiction with which we shackle ourselves.*

*You turn our setbacks into comebacks.*

*For that, we are grateful.*

*Even as we trust in your will, Lord,*

*we confess that we cannot always make sense of diseases that burden us;*

*we can't make sense of extreme wealth while people die in poverty;*

*we don't always know why bad things happen to those we love.*

*We confess that it is not always well with our souls. Sometimes the yoke feels too heavy to bear.*

*But we believe in resurrection, Lord.*

*We see it with every flower that breaks through a wintered ground*

*and with every rainbow that greets us in a storm.*

*We have experienced resurrection in our lives through your Son's powerful story.*

*Heal us; heal this world, we pray.*

*Heal us within your powerful will.*

*Amen.*

# Home

So "home" is not what you know;
it's not the familiar.
It comes from a deeper place.

—9 December 2008 Journal Entry

*However far the stream flows, it never forgets its source.*

—YORUBA OF NIGERIA PROVERB

hen I tell people that I'm from South Carolina, they inevitably ask me where I lived in the state. It's never been an easy answer. I went to three elementary schools, two middle schools, and three high schools in several different cities and regions of South Carolina. I've never called any particular place "home."

In fact, I've never quite known what to do with the idea of home. Now that my dad lives in New York City, a place where I've never lived, do I say that I'm going home for Christmas? Is home a place? Is it wherever the people you love are? Or is home more of a feeling? Since I never had a place in mind, it's always been more of a feeling to me.

So it surprised me when I met Helen in Liberia and heard her say, "It feels so good to be home." Helen was born in Monrovia, Liberia's capital city. Her family left the country when Helen was a year old, shortly before violence erupted with Samuel Doe's coup d'état. I lost count as she named the many countries where her family moved. Her accent was as American as mine, and she's spent a significant amount of her adulthood in Chicago. She has every reason to be as noncommittal as I am about identifying a "home," but she claims Liberia—a country whose soil her feet had not touched for more than thirty years until her recent return. She doesn't remember living in Liberia, but Liberia is home.

*Isaac remembers the* palm trees when he speaks of war.

He remembers not having any food to eat and having to hide in the jungle with his family. He remembers not knowing where some of his family members were and if they would return alive. And he remembers eating palm leaves or palm nuts and making palm butter because there was nothing more to eat for miles and miles that wouldn't cost at least a limb or a life.

When Isaac remembers having to leave his home, he remembers the palm trees.

PRAY WITH ELIZABETH

Our area is a very remote area.

And now we've got our land here, but we don't have a school.

So my prayer request is that we want our children educated. . . .

Next, I want to go into ministry. I need prayer for my ministry.

And my husband was killed in the war.

I need a God-fearing husband to stand by me in my ministry. That's my request.

—ELIZABETH

*I thought of home* a lot in Liberia. It was our last destination before returning to the States, so we all compared notes about what we looked forward to doing when we got back home. Most of it involved eating.

I was also reminded of home every time I saw Liberia's star and stripes flag that so closely resembles ours, when PB & J was a regular mealtime offering, or whenever someone said, "That will be $400 dollars" (Liberian dollars, of course, but it just felt like home to hear the word *dollar*). As the only

African country to be founded by the American Colonization Society, Liberians probably have more in common with the United States than other parts of the continent.

It seems like the idea of home has been one factor that sparked years of war in Liberia. Americo-Liberians, freed American slaves who had been sent to colonize the country, were primarily in power and control of the land, which took power away from indigenous people. Which group should lead and call Liberia home—the people whose ancestors were born there or the people whose ancestors returned to Africa and grew the country? I don't mean to trivialize the years-long civil war with this one question; certainly, it doesn't address all of the issues contributing to the war. The issue of who *owns* the land and who *controls* it underlies so many conflicts on the continent. It makes sense that this question still exists today when so much of the continent was colonized by foreigners who staked claim in someone else's backyard, bringing a new set of values, ideas, and systems. This underlying struggle continues to plague much of Africa. Who gets to claim the land?

I can't imagine being forced from a place I considered home because of a war on my soil. I became increasingly grateful that we haven't had a war inside the United States during my lifetime as we journeyed through Liberia and saw its war ruins—both physical and emotional. I became increasingly sad that people in some parts of the world are experiencing demise because of war—even this very minute—in a place they call home.

*When the rebels caught* Bishop Innis, they pistol-whipped him, gashing his head repeatedly. He and his family thought for sure that his days on earth were numbered. The entire family had to run for their lives when the rebels returned.

Bishop Innis was in Tubmanville, serving as director of the United Methodist Mission where he harbored more than three hundred children who had fled the fighting in other parts of the country. He fed and sheltered these children, offering them refuge from the ongoing civil war.

The rebels, who were young boys, did not like his work; so they let him know just how much they disliked it. Their attack on the mission station shut down the campus in 1993. Bishop Innis survived the attacks and eventually healed, but he had to leave Camphor and work in Monrovia. Many years and many homes later, Bishop Innis now funds the schooling for many young children in Buchanan, believing that

education will stop the cycle of conflict. He's even forgiven one of his attackers, offering him a standing invitation to come to him so that he can fund his education.

Bishop Innis is hoping that his homeland will study war no more.

*She named me Akoko.* As we prepared to return home, I recalled a conversation from Uganda. Benson translated as I spoke with the people of the Awer Internally Displaced Persons (IDP) camp in Uganda and laughed when he told me they were trying to come up with a new name for me. One man recommended Atim, which means "born outside homeland" in Acholi. Another said, "No! It should be Alal." This means "disappear to another land." I appreciated the emerging theme.

Eyes smiling, Vincentina looked directly into my eyes and said, "Your name is Akoko." Even though I didn't understand a word of Acholi, her eyes told me that the name she gave me was the one to choose.

Benson said that Akoko means "heart's cry." He asked Vincentina why she selected this name for me. She explained that I was born away from my homeland and that for so many years the heart of Africa has been crying out for me to return. She smiled and welcomed me home.

Home. I suppose every person of African descent born in the United States experiences the strange dichotomy of being both from Africa and from America. Even though I was born in a Georgia hospital, Africa was deep in my history long before I stood on her soil and even before I was conceived. This reality has shaped my family's history and our present.

I am also a product of the United States of America with all of its development, consumerism, education, freedom, and voice. So much of my story is informed by a way of life in a country so vastly different from nearly all countries in Africa.

And yet, Africa is my homeland.

Thank you for being constant throughout the ages.

When we are friendless, you are our friend.

When we are orphaned, you are our parent.

When we are peaceful, you are our peace.

When we are happy, you are our joy.

When we are homeless, you are our home.

*In this world you have given to us, homes are ravaged by war,*

*greed,*

*betrayal,*

*neglect.*

*You created us to care for one another. In so many ways, we have failed.*

*But we are grateful that you are still creating us.*

*You still call us to care for this home you've given to us,*

*and each day holds the promise of war's ending, greed's destruction,*

*betrayal's transformation, and neglect's restoration.*

*You show us ways to make sure every mouth is fed,*

*every child can learn, and every refugee can return home.*

*In you, Lord, we find our home. May our souls rest in you.*

*Amen.*

*I remember sitting at* the breakfast table one of our last days on the continent when Cary said, "I'm not sure I'm ready to go home." I was relieved to hear him say this because I had filled journal pages with this very thought the night before. While we could already taste the chicken sandwiches and burritos we had longed to eat for days and could not wait to wrap our arms around our families, there was something difficult about leaving. We were anxious for the joys of home, but we were leaving new friends who were living fully—even those who had death knocking on their doors.

We also faced a different reality at home. Cary's home had changed drastically while we were on the continent; he was returning to something new and unknown. For Austin, who left his job to come to Africa with us, being home meant that he was going to have to find his next way of paying the bills. I knew that home meant facing my everyday stressors, piled-up bills, and a decision about which parent I would visit for Christmas.

For all of us, going home meant saying good-bye to one another for a while. We had shared a story together, and this chapter was ending. We all knew we'd repeatedly hear the very innocent question, "How was your trip?," and wish we could wrap the answer in a tidy box and hand it to the inquisitor; but we weren't ready to do that yet. We knew that our adventure was ending but the incredible responsibility of distributing these prayers and building relationships across continents was only beginning.

On the flight home, I closed my eyes and tried to replay every moment of the journey. The concerns of those we were leaving behind were not like mine. I worried about bills and debts from acquiring both extravagant and necessary things. Sidibé worried about feeding his daughter. I worried about family relationships. Charlotte worried about whether her sister would live. But I did not feel the need to trivialize my hardships or glorify theirs. I did not feel guilty about our economic wealth or pity for their financial burdens. I did not feel sorry for our impoverished spirits or envy their abundant faith. The people I met did not pity or envy me. They simply lived one prayer at a time.

So I took a few deep breaths and reflected on some of the greatest lessons I learned while praying with Africa. We are all in this one world, desperate for survival. We can try to survive on our own, but we exist more vibrantly together. No matter how our joys or pains look, all of us can get through them one prayer at a time.

We need prayer—like breath and water. It keeps us alive.

## THE BEGINNING

arly in 2008, Cary Graham traveled to South Africa for the first time. He encountered an Africa that was not quite like the images the TV, magazines, and nonprofits had shown him. He met people with swollen hearts, not just swollen bellies. He saw people who were caring for their communities, not simply holding out hands for help. He realized that his picture of Africa was not entirely true-to-life for the broad scope, diversity, and reality of people on the entire African continent.

Cary hoped to find a way to dispel the images—the half-truths and stereotypes—people in the United States often have of Africans by allowing the people of Africa to speak for themselves. He thought that one of the best ways to do this was to ignite a conversation between people in the United States and people in various African countries through prayer. Even if groups do not pray in the same way or for the same things, Cary wanted the people of the world to hear each other's prayer requests and start praying *with* each other instead of just *for* each other. When we pray with someone, we enter into an intimate conversation with that person and with God, giving birth to a life-changing relationship.

This idea became PRAY WITH AFRICA. With the help of his friends, Ciona Rouse, a writer who also experienced the same reality during her 2005 visit to the continent, and Austin Flack, a filmmaker who had worked for various nonprofits focused on developing nations in Africa and other parts of the world, Cary fleshed out the PRAY WITH AFRICA idea. The trio decided to travel to several African countries, encounter the prayer requests of people there, and record their realities on film—both the pain and the joy. They brought these prayer requests back to the United States and are now inviting the world to join together in the most divine dialogue of all—prayer.

PRAY WITH AFRICA exists to inspire people to connect across continents, to pray each other's prayers, and to put those prayers into action.

Learn more about PRAY WITH AFRICA and join a worldwide prayer community: www.PrayWithAfrica.com.

# NOTES

## Introduction

1. Oswald Chambers, *My Utmost for His Highest: An Updated Edition in Today's Language,* ed. James Reimann (Grand Rapids, MI: Discovery House Publishers, 1992), October 17.

## Community

Epigraph from Desmond Tutu, *Believe: The Words and Inspiration of Desmond Tutu* (Boulder, CO: Blue Mountain Press, 2007), 5.

2. Oxfam America statistic: http://www.oxfamamerica.org/whatwedo/where_we_work/west_africa/news_publications/aja_mali/feature_story.2005-08-11.7895862723

## Patience

Epigraph from Oyekan Owomoyelap, *Yoruba Proverbs* (Lincoln, NE: University of Nebraska Press, 2005), 153.

## Forgiveness

Epigraph from Desmond Tutu with Douglas Abrams, *God Has a Dream: A Vision of Hope for Our Time* (New York: Doubleday, 2004), 43.

3. Pamela and Stella are being restored through the Zion Project Ministry for young women in Gulu, Uganda: www.zionproject.org

## Healing

Epigraph from Julia Stewart, *African Proverbs and Wisdom: A Collection for Every Day of the Year from More Than Forty African Nations* (Secaucus, N.J.: Carol Publishing, 1998), 159.

## Home

Epigraph, Ibid., 15.